# SLOWEDOWNLIGHT

**Albums**
**One & Two**

**Song Lyrics**
**By**
**Michael van Himbergen**
**&**
**Richard Murrieta**

©2014

For information, address:
Enlightening Publishers, LLC
105 Eototo Road, El Prado, NM 87529
Email: publishers@icloud.com

First Edition
1 2 3 4 5 6 7 8 9 0
Printed in the United States of America
Library of Congress Cataloging-in-Publication Data
Michael A. Van Himbergen, 1953
ISBN 13-9781505552614
ISBN 10-1505552613
(Identity: Rock & Roll Lyrics)
Visit www.enlighteningpublishers.com
Email: publishers@icloud.com
Email: contactmvh@gmail.com

# FALLING

Feels like we're falling again
Watching the weather
Hoping to win
Yet not quite women
Yet not quite men
Feels like we're falling again.

Slip away, son, get away, run away from Babylon, man.
Walk away, friends. Drive away.
Fly away, sail away, get away from Babylon, mate.
When Babylon falls, it will fall on a very nice day.

When we were young, so young
When we first heard of Babylon, man.
It was wondrous. Had everything we dreamed.

Now walk away, friend. Run away from Babylon, man.
Drive away, crawl away.

Sirens singing:
I am OK. I'm in L.A. I am OK. I'm in L.A. I am OK. I'm in L.A. I am OK.
I'm in there, baby.

Just like the TV, you and me.
We're just like the TV, you and me.
Feels like we're falling.
Feels like we're falling again.

When we were young, so young
When we first heard of Babylon, man.
It was wondrous, had everything we dreamed.

Now walk away, friend. Run away.
Drive away now. Walk away, crawl away.

Feels like we're falling again
Watching the weather
Hoping to win.

Feels like we're falling.
Feels like we're falling.

# RABBIT MAN

Fuck it
It's a drop in the bucket
Yeah you should chuck it
Back into the sea.

As luck would have it
I got trapped like a rabbit
I had to naw my foot off
To be free
To be free

I'm gonna live on the broken highway
I've got a couple old lovers out there
I'm gonna run gonna run with the Rabbit Roamads
I'm gonna run, run, run

Warren to warren
I'm smoking' CandyMan Brand, man
I'm gonna live under the broken sky
And leave my mark and my generation
The mark of Rabbit Man

Fuck it
It's a drop in the bucket
Yeah you should chuck it
Back into the sea.

There'll be a man there
He'll understand
He'll tell you chuck it
Back into the sea

I'm gonna live on the broken highway
I've got a couple old lovers out there
I'm gonna run gonna run with the Rabbit Roamads
I'm gonna run, run, run

Warren to warren
I'm smoking' CandyMan Brand, man
I'm gonna live under the broken sky
And leave my mark and my generation
The mark of Rabbit Man

As luck would have it
I got trapped like a rabbit
I had to naw my foot off
To be free
To be free

Fuck it
It's a drop in the bucket
Yeah you should chuck it
Back into the sea

# TAKE IT BACK

I bought an interactive TV
It turns on when I clap
Imagine that, baby

But after three weeks of messing with it
I took it back
And bought a European vacuum cleaner
I took it back to
And bought a Japanese wobbulator
Took that back

I fill my life up with crap
To hell with that
Take it back
Tack it back
Take it all back

Said I loved your cowgirl outfit
I even liked yer hat
Well I take that back
I said whole lot of things about you
Behind your back, darling

Did I say I'd sell my condo for you
Well I take that back now
At least a I never cheated on you
I take that back

I fill my life up with crap
To hell with that
Take it back
To hell with that
Tack it back
Take it back
Take it all back

Said I'd sell my soul to Jesus
For a million dollars cash
But he wouldn't buy that
I tried the same deal with Satan
Except for he wants the cash back

Did I say I never hurt nobody
Well I take that back to
Hey at least I never killed no one
At least not yet

I fill my life up with crap
To hell with that
Take it back
Tack it back
Tack it back
Take it all back
Take it back

# CYBERCLONES

We are dancing in the light again
Channeling our twins
Here we go again we're not alone
We got our cyberclones

Every click you make
Every heart you break
They'll be watching
And replicating

Everything we buy
Till' the day we die
Fills the happy homes
Of our cyberclones

We are dancing in the light again
Channeling our friends
Here we go again we're not alone
Not with our cyberclones

Everywhere we go
We're on video
So the clones can grow
And run the whole the damn show

No matter what we know
About the Roamad Code
Deep in the webgridz
Live our cyberclones

We'll be dancing in the light again
Channeling our twins
Here we go again we're not alone
We've got our cyberclones

Every click you make
Every heart you break
They'll be watching
Replicating

# WHAT I WOULDN'T DO

Well what I wouldn't do
Is lay that trip on you
About a man-machine
A man-machine interface

Oh oh oh oh yeah
Oh oh oh oh oooo yeah

I wouldn't lay that trip on you about man-machine interface
With a neuro-muscular tracking pattern of a cat's eye
Combined with a return-turret-head swing movement

Thermographic CRT scope
Filthy village sleepy with jungle
Long grown over run-way
Old man drunk with war stories
Mutilated girl-child squatting in the afternoon dust
Like a big pink frog
Oh yeah

Well what I wouldn't do
Is lay that trip on you
About a man-machine
A man-machine interface

Man-machine interface
Oh yeah
Oh oh ah ah oh yeah

Meanwhile go around dumping bucks, supplies, personal, equipment
Helicopter swims overhead long enough to see its hooked-lined underbelly
1972 Cadillac landing on her back like a meteor from the mouth of God

Well what I would not do
Is lay that trip on you
About a man-machine
A man-machine interface

# STARLAMP

Starlamp
Under the starlamp
Under the starlamp
Under the starlamp
Under the starlamp

Everything turns surreal
The language, the look, the feel
Everybody knows your name
The fans will fan the flames of fame
The fans will fan the flames of fame

Everything changes
Everything changes fast
Faces rearrange
It started underneath the starlamp

Under the starlamp
Under the starlamp
Under the starlamp

Frozen boys lick their lips
Frozen girls quip their quips
There's money and chicks for free
Herostratus and Ziggy

Everything is changing
Everything changes fast
Faces rearrange
It freezing underneath the starlamp

Under the starlamp
Under the starlamp
Under the starlamp
Under the starlamp
Under the starlamp

Go ahead suck it and see
There's Janet and Kurt and Jimmy
With Marc and Pink and Marley
And one day baby you and me

Under the starlamp
Under the starlamp

Under the starlamp
Under the starlamp

Everything looks surreal
The language, the feel
Everybody knows your name
The fans will fan the flames of fame
The fans will fan the flames of fame

Under the starlamp

# WAYBACKINTHENIGHT

©2014 Michael van Himbergen & Richard Murrieta

Just like the others
It's filled with your brothers
It's filled with your sisters
From other lands

The others get what your brothers deserve
The friend you put on shelf remembers
All the cool old secrets of light

Waybackinthenight
Waybackinthenight
Waybackinthenight
Waybackinthenight

We started something bubbling back there
We should have never have started at all, allright?
We started something nectronic baby

Waybackinthenight
Waybackinthenight
Waybackinthenight
Waybackinthenight

You really got me
You really got me going
You really got me going

Hey! What's the matter with you?
I'm in you. Your in me
I'm in you. Your in me
I'm in you. Your in me
I'm in you. Your in me
I'm in you. Your in me
I'm in you. Your in me

Waybackinthenight
Waybackinthenight
Waybackinthenight
Waybackinthenight

And just like the others
It's filled with your brothers
It's filled with your sisters
From other lands

The others get what your brothers deserve
The friend you put on shelf remembers

Waybackinthenight
Waybackinthenight
Waybackinthenight
Waybackinthenight

Hey! What's the matter with you?
I'm in you. You're in me
I'm in you. You're in me
I'm in you. You're in me
I'm in you. You're in me
Hey! What's the matter with you?
I'm in you. You're in me
I'm in you. You're in me
I'm in you. You're in me

# HINGES ON THE HUMAN HEART

We never want to desert you
We always tried to support you
We always talked about that
We always talked about that
We always told you

It all hinges on the human heart
Glowing in the darkness
It all hinges on the human heart
Together or apart
It all hinges with the human heart

A whole of people walking round talking about
A universe of spiraling darkness
They'll be sucking all the juice out of everything and everyone
Ripping our lives apart

Saying, we never wanted to hurt you
We allways wanted to help
We always talked about that
We always talked about that
We always you that it all

Hinges on the human heart
Glowing in the darkness
It all hinges on the human heart
Together or apart
It all hinges with the human heart

A whole of people walking round talking about
A universe of spiraling darkness
They'll be sucking all the juice out of everything and everyone
Ripping our lives apart

Saying, we never wanted to hurt you
We always wanted to help
We always talked about that
We always talked about that
We always told you it all

It all hinges on the human heart
Glowing in the darkness
It all hinges on the human heart
Together or apart

It all hinges with the human heart
It all hinges with the human heart
Glowing in the darkness

# DRIVE ME HOME  ©2014 Michael van Himbergen

We went to eat out at some tacky Bistros
You had gazpacho and I had fish too

The night is blown
Drive me home
The night is blown
Drive me home

You're all ways criticizing me about the way I spend my leisure time
Well you and your affluhip friends make me want to puke

Work and eat and screw and sleep there ain't no more, baby
Believe it
There ain't no more

'Cause every day's an endless stream
Of cigarettes and magazines
And every strangers face I see
Reminds me that I want to be with you

You and your chic ideas, Baja health spa
You got pneumonia
And I got sick too

The trip is blown
Fly me home
The trip is blown
Fly me home

You're all ways criticizing me about the way I spend my leisure time
Well you and your affluhip friends make me want to puke
Work and eat and screw and sleep there ain't no more, baby
Believe it
Believe it

'Cause every strangers face I see
Reminds me that I want to be with you
Reminds me that I want to be with you

# SCIENCE IS SUCH SWEET SORROW

I call you up
Room 23
You tell me
Meet me in the lobby
Don't let on you know me
Ask me for a match

And if you're followed home
Take your pill pull the phone
Remember this is war this is war this is war
Remember this is war this is war this is war

My friends and me are hungry
Please which ways the café?
Yeah we've got some money
Here? Just for a few days
Troubles with the language
Have you got that match?

And if you're followed home
Take your pill pull the phone
Remember this is war this is war this is war
Remember this is war this is war this is war

My dear, science is such sweet sorrow
With philosophical-technolo-Jesus
Tomorrow's gonna be
Nirvana-cum-satori
We won't need no more Feelies
We're way before your time
We're way before your time
We're way before your time

My dear, bite into such sweet sorrow
While your wobulating in your sleep
Tomorrow's gonna be
The epic of ITV
The Sacred Book of Naughty
So where the hell was mommy?
She wanted nothing more
So daddy bought the store
Good thing your records' clean

We're way before your time
We're way before your time
We're way before your time

Someone take that guy out and shoot him
He's just a sycophant
A dyslexic sycophant
Take him out shoot him, man
Take him out and shoot

I lay down
I close that hatch with my foot
Factories shut down under my tissues
I call your number

Guess we had a rotten childhood
Guess we had a rotten childhood
Guess we had a rotten childhood

I get up fast
And walk out past ITV
Like chemical sequences dripping with face fluids
Switching drugs
Switching drugs
Switching drugs
Switching drugs
Switching drugs

Rolling oceans of digital oxygen
Rolling oceans of digital oxygen
Rolling oceans of digital oxygen
Rolling oceans of digital oxygen

Plants like me
Plants like me
You mean all this time I've been unthinkingly
Holding myself up and down in the way that I move?
Big quiet gardens with plants like me
Big quiet gardens with plants like me

Guess we had a rotten childhood
Guess we had a rotten childhood
In the back rooms of our memory
Of our hometown output

My dear, science is such sweet sorrow

# READY SET STOP

©2014 Michael van Himbergen/ Lyrics by Richard Murrieta

I'm a little under the weather
But I won't be forever
I'm standing on the platform, baby
Don't pull the lever
Don't pull the lever

You know we started on this endeavor
We almost had it together
My moves were getting smooth, baby
You used to say I was clever

But there won't be no gallows fodder
Spinning like a top
Locked up in your bell jar, baby
I think I'm gonna pop

Like ready set stop
You can push me to the side
Just don't pull me off the top
Don't pull me off the top

Like ready set stop
Ready set stop

I'm broke up inside, baby
What did you have to dis me for
Go ahead and leave lover
Go walk out that door

Stop
Ready set stop
Stop ready set stop

I'm a little under the weather
But I won't be forever
You use to say I was clever

Just don't pull me off the top

# UNDERNEATH THE TABLE

©2014 Michael van Himbergen. Lyrics by Richard Murrieta

Underneath the table
Underneath the table
Underneath the table
Underneath

If you want to do her
Don't W2 her
If you really like the way she looks
Keep it off the books

If you want to get ahead
Better keep it from the feds
Don't report her income
If want to get some

If you do this for her
She will make you stable
She'll dress like Betty Grable
Underneath the table

You know she's an actress
Because she likes the practice
She'll even work late nights
Dressed up in black tights

She's gotta pay for classes
That's why she's washing glasses
Gotta pay for coaching
Gotta pay for Motrin

If you do this for her
She will make you stable
She'll dress like Betty Grable
Underneath the table

Taking care of business for you won't make her sad
It's easy 'cause she like you
You remind her of her dad
Just like her dad

She can stalk the back bar
She can count the cash
Keep 'em happy four-deep
Tacking out the trash

It's a simple trade off
Maybe just a shade off
Just no paid off or laid off
None of that
If you want to do her
Don't W2 her
If you really like the way she looks
Keep it off the books

Keep it underneath the table
Underneath the table

# GO AHEAD AND CALL THE COPS

©2014 Michael van Himbergen. Lyrics by Richard Murrieta

Go ahead and call the cops
Go ahead

You were crazy when I met you
You're crazy even now
But I still love you, baby

You and I ching like the dow
You and I ching like the dow

My stuff is scattered everywhere
You're locked up in the Lou
Well what am I supposed to do
You're locked up in the Lou
What am I supposed to do

You and I ching like the dow
You and I ching like the dow

Go ahead and call the cops
Go ahead
Go ahead and call the cops
Go ahead
Go ahead and call the cops

My stuff is scattered everywhere
You're locked up in the Lou
Eh' what am I supposed to do
You're locked up in the Lou

Got the phone in there, baby?

You and I ching like the dow
Let me in there
You and I ching like the dow

Go ahead and call the cops
Go ahead
911, baby
Go ahead

Hey, I ain't gonna hurt you
I only want to talk
Just want to talk, baby

Knock knock
Common, baby
Go ahead
Go ahead and call the cops
Don't break no fingernail there baby when you dial

# WASH AWAY MY SINS

©2014 Michael van Himbergen Lyrics by Richard Murrieta

I had sex with an old school friend of mine last night
Still trying to decide if it was wrong or right
That's why I seem so distant today
Trying decide if I should go or I should stay

Wash away my sins in the dreams of another man, baby
Wash away my sins in the streams of another man, baby
Wash away my sins in the screams of another man, baby

I know I love you but I can't bring myself to say
You're the only that can make me feel a certain way

If I had it all to do again maybe I'd climb a mountain
Maybe just fly away

Wash away my sins in the dreams of another man
Wash away my sins in the screams of another man
And another and another and another

You see, there's so many dreams I haven't told you
This is just a little piece
I can't help but feeling you got just as much at least

When you remind me of all you've thrown away
There's a weight that get released
I know I don't have to stay

Just knowing that its coming makes me happy I been bad
I anticipate the heart ache and look forward to the sad
Realize now
You gotta

Wash away my sins in the dreams of another man
Wash away my sins in the screams of another man
Wash away my sins in the streams of another man
Wash away my sins

# JIMMY

I'm telling Jimmy
I'm telling Jimmy
I'm telling Jimmy
All about you
I'm telling

I'm telling Jimmy
I'm telling Jimmy
I'm telling Jimmy
All about you
I'm telling

Jimmy told me
Life's so grand
When you're an angry man

Jimmy told me
Life's so grand
When you're an angry man
I'm telling

I'm telling Jimmy
I'm telling Jimmy
All about you
I'm telling

If I tell Jimmy what I just saw
It's gonna piss him off
He'll blow on over in his daddy's car
And knock your stupid head off

I'm telling Jimmy
I'm telling
I'm telling

Ain't it a shame nobody digs nobody serious
Ain't it a shame
Ain't it a shame nobody digs nobody seriously
Ain't it a shame nobody digs no one
Ain't it a shame nobody takes nobody seriously

Jimmy told me
Life's so grand
When you're an angry man
I'm telling

If I tell Jimmy what I just saw
It's gonna piss him off
He'll blow on over in his daddy's car
And knock your stupid head off

# GONE ON GONE

Gone on gone
Gone on gone

I've held a dying lover in my arms
And just to think she'll never hold another moment
A dream gone on gone

I've held a dying lover in my arms
And just to think she'll never hold another moment
A dream gone on gone

Gone on gone
Gone on gone
Dream gone on gone
Dream gone on gone
Dream gone on gone
Dream gone on gone
Dream gone on gone

I've held a dying lover in my arms
And just to think she'll never hold another moment
I've always thought that love would never die
But now I see it's just an ordinary moment
A dream gone on gone

Dream gone on gone
Dream gone on gone
Dream gone on gone
Gone on gone
Gone on gone

# TWENTY OH ONE

Twenty oh one
Twenty oh one
Remember twenty oh one
911

Take off the gold
Loose the gun
Kill the fear
Grow the love
Kill the fear
Grow the love
Grow the love

Yo, I'm a white boy
Not quite the right boy
To be shouting out gratis
But it seems we've all been co-opted
Adopted by the quo bro
Sold out status
Sold out status

Twenty oh one
Kill the fear
Remember twenty oh one
We need some new tactics here

Not sure the metaphor
Of the Pimp and the Whore
Is effective anymore

Brag rapper LLC
Yo, fleshy billboard
Corporate logo with legs ace
Endorser, posturer, poser
Maken that tough guy face

Take off the gold
Loose the gun
Kill the fear
Grow the love

Why keep grabbing at das manhood
Got the clap or something real good?
Mayhap need to wee wee

Yo momma got el pee pee
Supposed to be tantalizing?
Enlightenizing?

Take off the gold
Remember twenty oh one
Twenty oh one
Kill the fear
Grow the love
Kill the fear
Grow the love

The only message that makes it through the system
Is the futility of any meaningful resistance
Is the worship of the shallowest materialistic existence

Is the dehumanization of women who are our best friends

Remember twenty oh one
Twenty oh one
Kill the fear
Grow the love
Kill the fear
Grow the love

While we were otherwise distracted
They got us exactly where they want us
We're gonna need some new tactics here
Politically neutralized
Socio-economically commoditized
Alienated from ourselves and each other
Ultimately we've got about as much buzz
As a plastic action figure rotting in some French fries 'cuz

Twenty oh one

Take off the gold
Loose the gun
Grow the love

# BLURRY

Let's go out and play
First check the weather
Says it's blurry out there

It's gonna get blurry
Blurry out there

Off to work you say
First check the threat, dear
Says it's blurry out there

It's getting real blurry
Blurry out there

On the internet
On the freeway
It's just a blurr, just a blurr
All the chatter
Lots of noise
Oh my God
It's all a blurr
It's all a blurr
It's all a blurr

It's getting real blurry
Blurry out there

Let's go out and pray
First check your weapons
It's probably blurry out there
Guess we better hurry
It's getting blurry out there

Blurry
Blurry out there

We the people of the United States
In order to form a more perfect union
Establish justice
Insure domestic tranquility
Provide for the common defense
Promote the general welfare

Secure the blessings of liberty
To ourselves and our prosperity
To ordain and establish this constitution
For the United States of America

It looks fast standing still
Just a blurr like the fool on the hill
On the TV it's getting blurry out there
It's getting way blurry
It' getting blurry out there
Oh my God it's all a blurr
It's getting blurry
Everywhere
Blurry out there

# ETERNAL HOLIDAY

We've got your man in there
We've got your brother there too
We've got your mother
Your sister and you

We got your boss in there
We've got your coworkers too
You'll take the martyrs vow
Or we'll kill them all now
You know we know how

We've got your man in there
We've got your man in there

Listen now
You take a train into the city
Pick up a truck from our friends
Drive up beside that lovely building
You'll be in paradise then
Then all this bloodshed will end my brothers
And the fun will begin
Worlds without end
Holiday

Eternal Holiday
Eternal Holiday
Eternal Holiday
Such a Holiday

Eternal Holiday
Eternal Holiday
Eternal Holiday
Such a Holiday

Listen now
When you get to the point
Make sure you've gone to the bathroom
Hit redial on you cell phone
Put a little piece of wood down in between your teeth
Bite real hard
Don't talk to anyone you see

We've got your man in there
You know what that means
We've got your man in there
We've got your brother there too
We've got your mother
Your sister and you

We've got your boss in there
We've got your coworkers too
You'll take the martyrs vow
Or we'll kill them right now

We've got your boss in there
We've got you dog in there too
We've got your man in there
And we know what to do
This is all 'cause of you

We've got your man in there
We've got him

# REMEMBER THE FUTURE NOW
©2014 Michael van Himbergen

We can remember the future
We can remember the future

Yeah it's gonna get better
Then it gonna get worse
With small amounts of water there at first

Yeah it's gonna get better
Then it's gonna get worse, worse, much worse
'Cause everybody's covered by the curse

Wrapping around our screens
Dancing inside our jeans
Like Don Quixote riding on a dinosaur
Like Don Quixote hideously lost
Riding on an dinosaur

Hey what do you do with a guy like that?
You suck out your teeth
Pull out your tongue or worse
Give into the curse
Give into the curse

The future
The future
We can remember the future the future the future
We can remember the future the future
We can remember the future

Yeah it's gonna get better
Then it gonna get worse
With small amounts of water there at first

Yeah it's gonna get better
Then it's gonna get worse, worse much worse
'Cause everybody's covered by the curse
'Cause everybody's covered by the curse

Wrapping around our screens
Dancing inside our jeans
Like Don Quixote riding on a dinosaur
Like Don Quixote hideously lost
Riding on an dinosaur

Hey what do you do with a guy like that?
You suck out your teeth
Pull out your tongue or worse
The future

You can remember the future the future
You can remember the future the future
Now

# SAINT MILTON

©2014 Michael van Himbergen

Was just a little boy
His daddy beat him bad 'ya hear
Locked him in a trailer out back
For 27 years

The church people found him
In the summer of love, dear
Been living at grandma's house
A good 40 years

We called him Saint Milton
We was just children
Nana said he was nuts
That he had gone bananas
Living like that
Living like that

He works in the garden out back
Walks by the railroad track
By the time he was sixty-one
He'd forgiven everyone

Out with the dog on the porch
Twinkle in his eye
Singing with the choir tonight
'Saints of the Blue Sky'

We called him Saint Milton
We was just children
Nana said he was nuts
That he had gone bananas
Living like that
Living like that

Was just a little boy
His daddy beat him bad 'ya hear
Locked him in a trailer out back
For 27 years

He works in the garden out back
Walks by the railroad track
By the time he was sixty-one
He'd forgiven everyone

We called him Saint Milton
We was just children
Nana said he was nuts
That he had gone bananas
Living like that
Living like that

Saint Milton

# About the Writers...

**Michael van Himbergen** was born in Hollywood, raised in Los Angeles, and graduated from California Institute of the Arts (CalArts Film & Video). Michael worked as a visual effects producer on films including *Spaceballs, Die Hard, Michael Jackson's Black or White, Stargate, What Dreams May Come* (Academy Award VFX) and others. Van Himbergen has written *OVERBLOWN* as a novel and screenplay. IMDB Internet Movie Database:

http://www.imdb.com/name/nm0887121/?ref=fn_al_nm_2

**Richard Murrieta** was born in Mesa, Arizona, and is currently a Data Engineer in New York. Rick has worked in data acquisition and analysis for many years but also enjoys writing poetry and lyrics for fun.